Do You Know the Moon?

Written and Illustrated by
Maura Corey

MW01539209

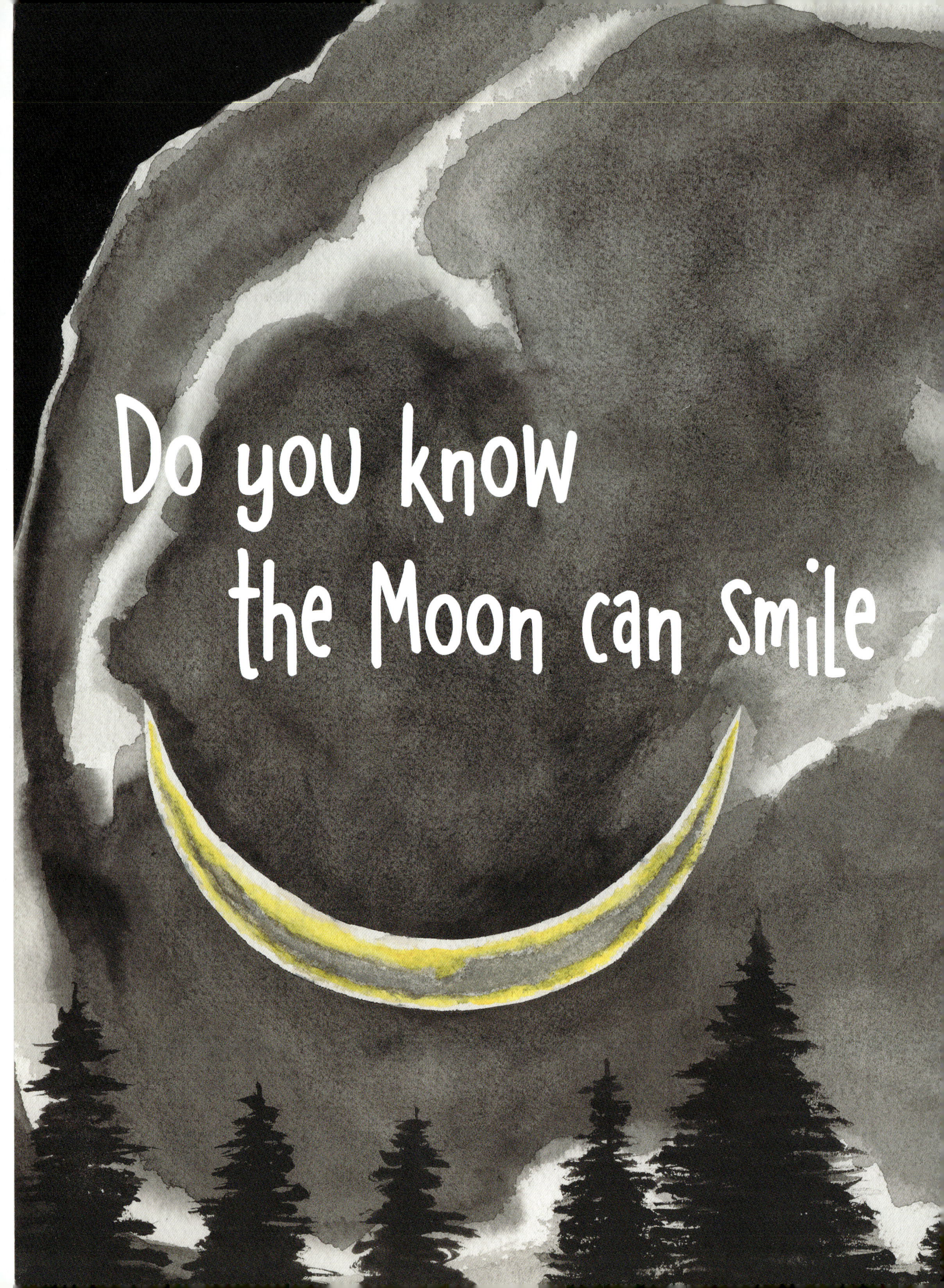

Do you know the Moon can smile

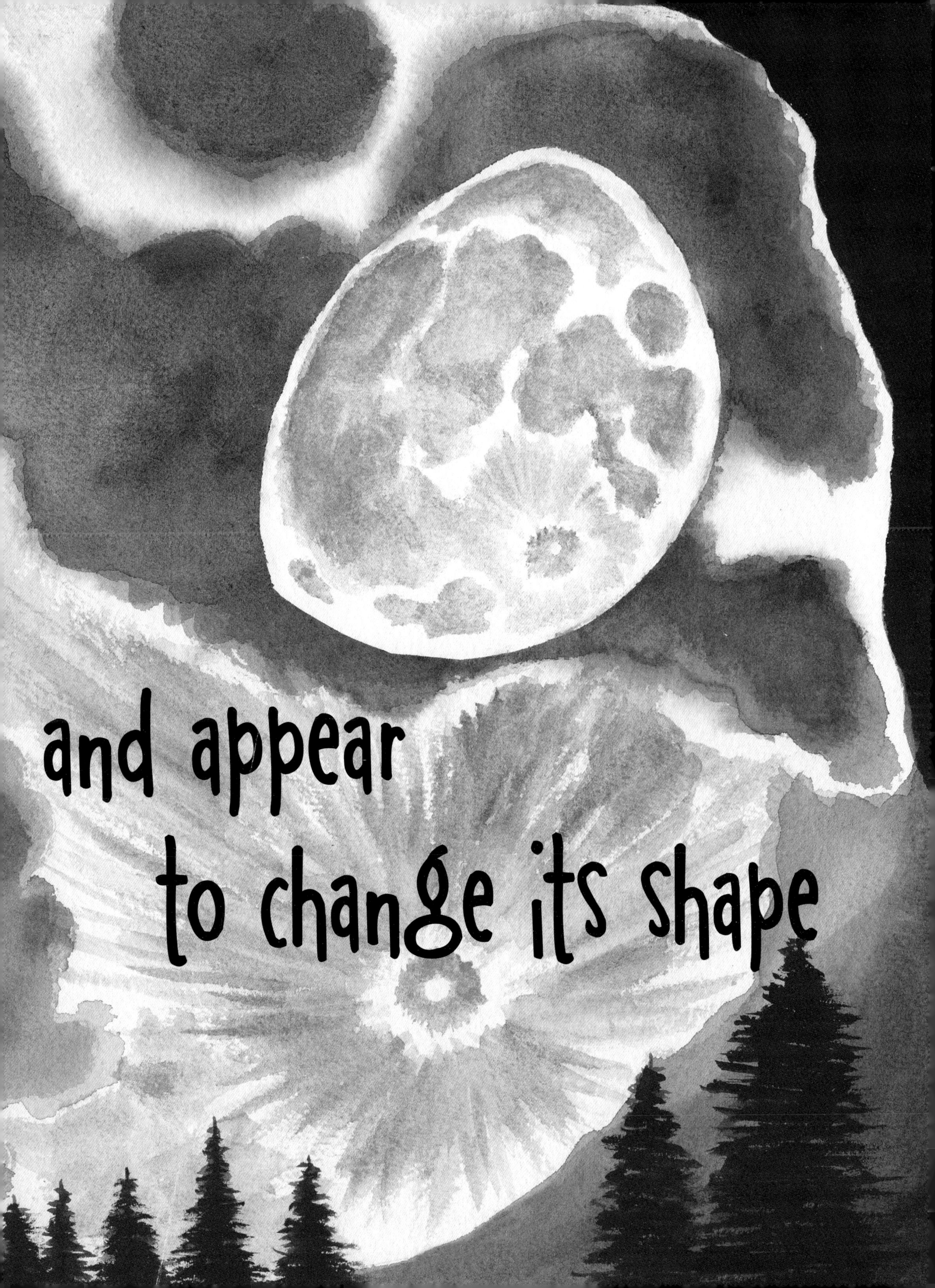

and appear
to change its shape

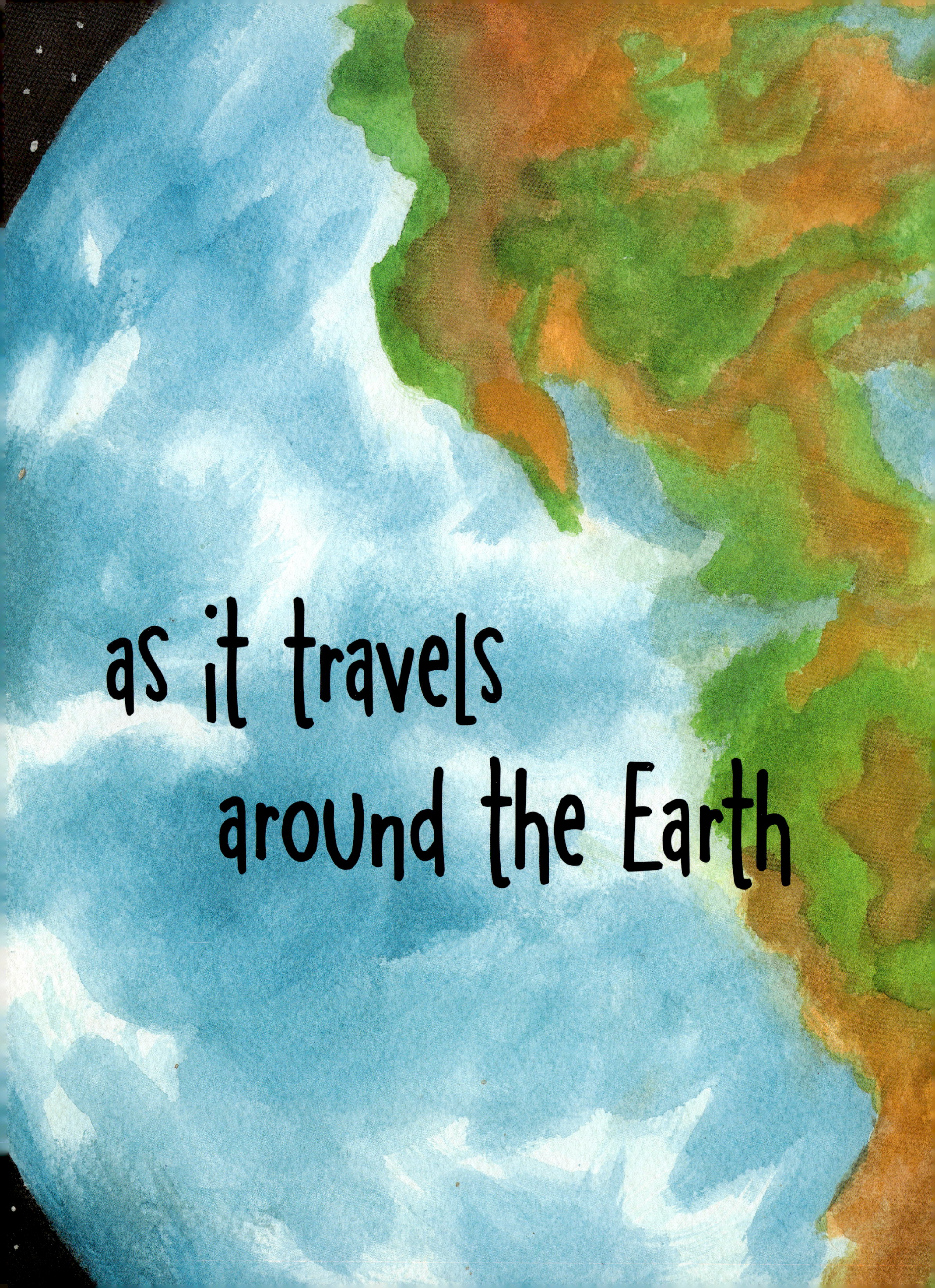

as it travels
around the Earth

and sunshine
lights its face?

Sometimes the Moon rises early.

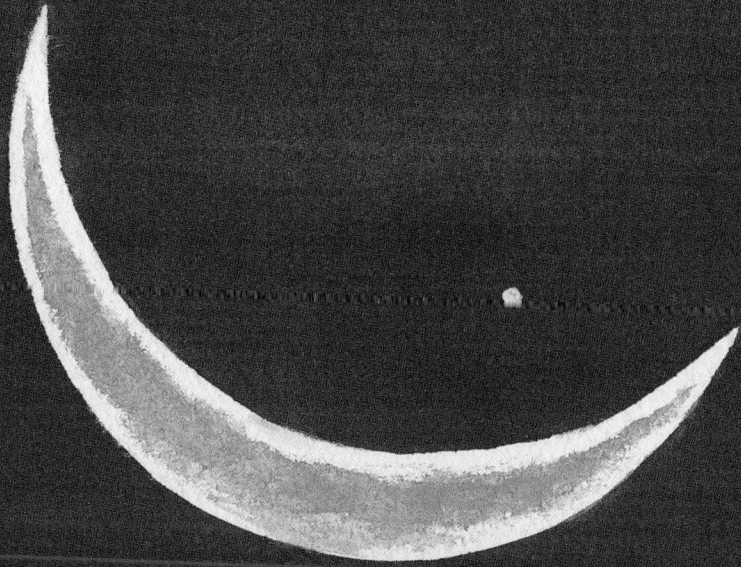

other nights
it's very late.

You see
this in the sky.

from Earth
to outer space.

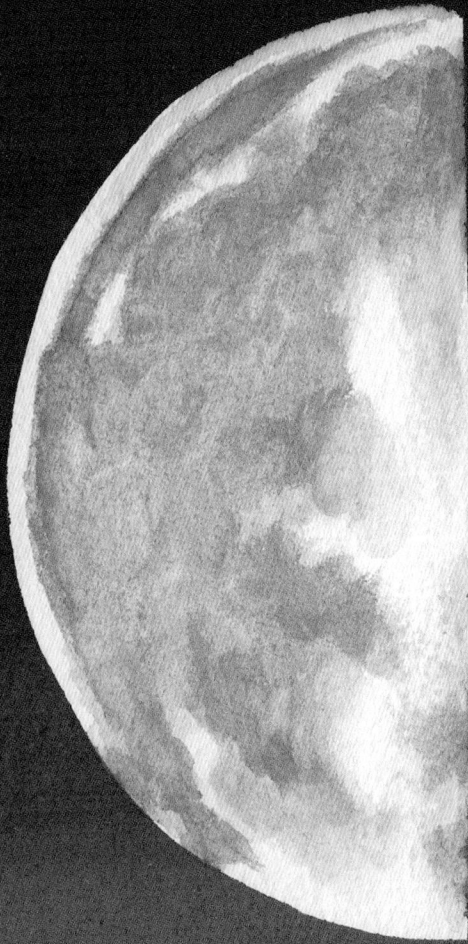

The Moon may look cut in half.

This phase is called a quarter.

Often when
you think it's full,
it's just a tad bit shorter.

I like it best
when big and round

with shadows

on the ground,

just like
in the daytime

these
shadows

follow me
around.

As the Sun
comes up each morning,
the Moon
may be in sight.

But in the dark
of evening it's best
to view this light.

except when the Moon
appears to hide,

the way
it did last night.

The sky was clear,

but all I saw
were stars ...

and stars ...

and stars ...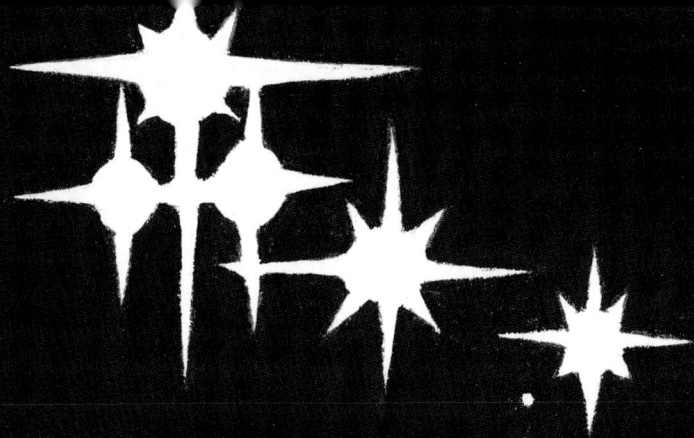

shining

ever oh so bright!

Do you know the Moon

can smile

and stay awake
while you lie down?

A light,
a guide,
a peaceful
sight ...

the Moon
wants to be found!